PRO WRESTLING'S GREATEST
MATCHES

BY MATT SCHEFF

SportsZone

An Imprint of Abdo Publishing
abdopublishing.com

abdopublishing.com

Published by Abdo Publishing, a division of ABDO, PO Box 398166, Minneapolis, Minnesota 55439. Copyright © 2017 by Abdo Consulting Group, Inc. International copyrights reserved in all countries. No part of this book may be reproduced in any form without written permission from the publisher. SportsZone™ is a trademark and logo of Abdo Publishing.

Printed in the United States of America, North Mankato, Minnesota
102016
012017

 THIS BOOK CONTAINS
RECYCLED MATERIALS

Cover Photo: Ron Elkman/Sports Imagery/Getty Images Sport/Getty Images
Interior Photos: Ron Elkman/Sports Imagery/Getty Images Sport/Getty Images, 1; Max Blain/ Shutterstock Images, 4-5, 6-7; Sam Aronov/Shutterstock Images, 8; Marc Serota/WWE/AP Images, 9, 16-17; Bruce Bennett Studios/Getty Images, 10-11; JP Yim/Getty Images Entertainment/Getty Images, 12-13; Yukio Hiraku/AFLO/Newscom, 14-15; Ricky Minton/Shutterstock Images, 15; Matt Roberts/ZumaPress/Newscom, 18-19, 22, 26-27, 28; Leonard Ortiz/ZumaPress/Newscom, 20-21; Jeff Siner/The Charlotte Observer/AP Images, 23; ZumaPress/Icon Sportswire, 24-25; Rick Scuteri/AP Images, 29

Editor: Patrick Donnelly
Series Designer: Laura Polzin

Publisher's Cataloging-in-Publication Data
Names: Scheff, Matt, author.
Title: Pro wrestling's greatest matches / by Matt Scheff.
Description: Minneapolis, MN : Abdo Publishing, 2017. | Series: Pro wrestling's
    greatest | Includes bibliographical references and index.
Identifiers: LCCN 2016945668 | ISBN 9781680784961 (lib. bdg.) |
    ISBN 9781680798241 (ebook)
Subjects: LCSH: Wrestling--Juvenile literature.
Classification: DDC 796.812--dc23
LC record available at http://lccn.loc.gov/2016945668

TABLE OF CONTENTS

INTRODUCTION: INTO THE RING

The lights dim. The music blares. The crowd goes wild as the wrestlers make their way to the mat for the main event.

What makes a great pro wrestling match? It's a combination of things. The wrestlers involved, the story lines, and the action in the ring all come together to make a match great.

The crowd roars at a tag-team match.

The buildup to the match is a big part of the excitement. Story lines and rivalries often stretch over months or even years. Bitter rivals battle it out for title belts or just pride.

Even more important is the action itself. The greatest matches are back-and-forth battles. Wrestlers execute their signature moves perfectly. They make narrow escapes. And they finish it off in a way that leaves fans thrilled—or heartbroken.

Fans love the high-flying action in a great match.

TEN

THE ROCK vs JOHN CENA (2012)

The WrestleMania 28 bout between The Rock and John Cena was long overdue. Cena was the fans' favorite babyface. The rivalry had been building for more than a year.

The Rock dominated early. But Cena stormed back. Cena tried to put The Rock away by using his opponent's own signature move—The People's Elbow. But The Rock was ready for it. He hit Cena with a Rock Bottom slam and it was over.

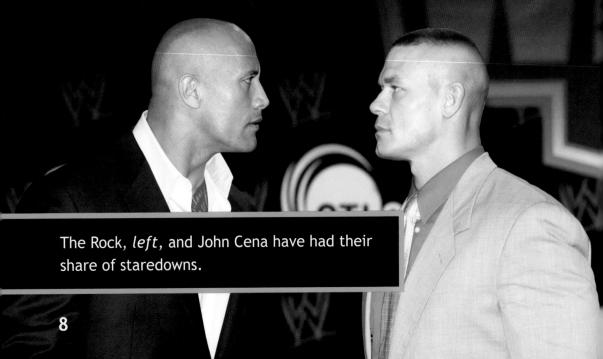

The Rock, *left*, and John Cena have had their share of staredowns.

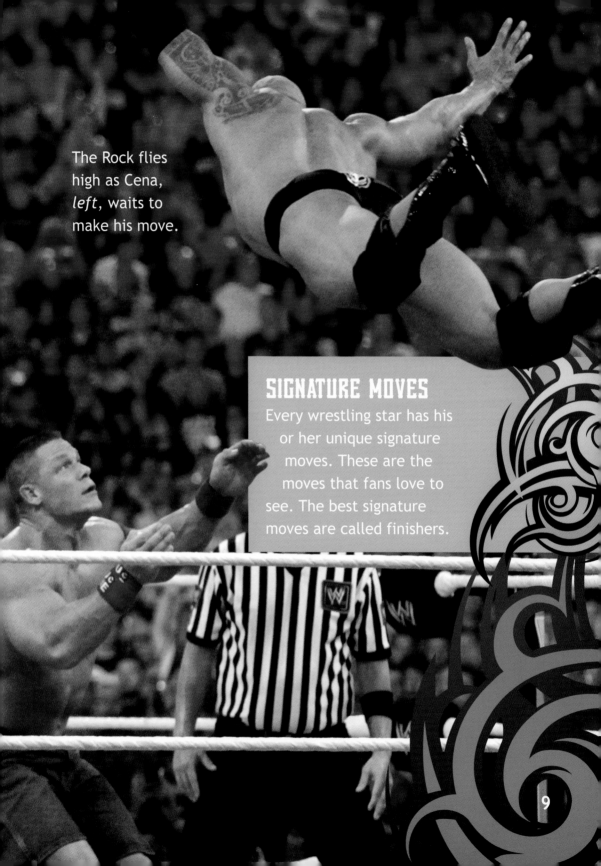

The Rock flies high as Cena, *left*, waits to make his move.

SIGNATURE MOVES

Every wrestling star has his or her unique signature moves. These are the moves that fans love to see. The best signature moves are called finishers.

NINE

1992 ROYAL RUMBLE

The World Wrestling Entertainment (WWE) World Heavyweight title was up for grabs. Thirty wrestlers were ready to stake their claim. They'd battle in a new type of match—a Royal Rumble. They entered the ring one at a time. The third wrestler to enter was an all-time great heel, Ric Flair. He lasted more than an hour in the ring. When Flair finally threw Sid Justice, the last remaining opponent, from the ring, it was over. Flair was the new champ.

Just about anything can happen in a Royal Rumble match.

11

EIGHT

BROCK LESNAR vs THE UNDERTAKER (2015)

The Undertaker was out for revenge in 2015. A year before, Brock Lesnar had ended The Undertaker's unbeaten streak at WrestleMania 30. The two giants entered the steel cage to battle one last time. It was a brutal, bloody match. Lesnar ripped part of the mat away, revealing the wood beneath. Then he slammed The Undertaker into the boards and covered him for a thrilling pin.

The Undertaker, *right*, had the upper hand early, but Brock Lesnar eventually turned the tables on him.

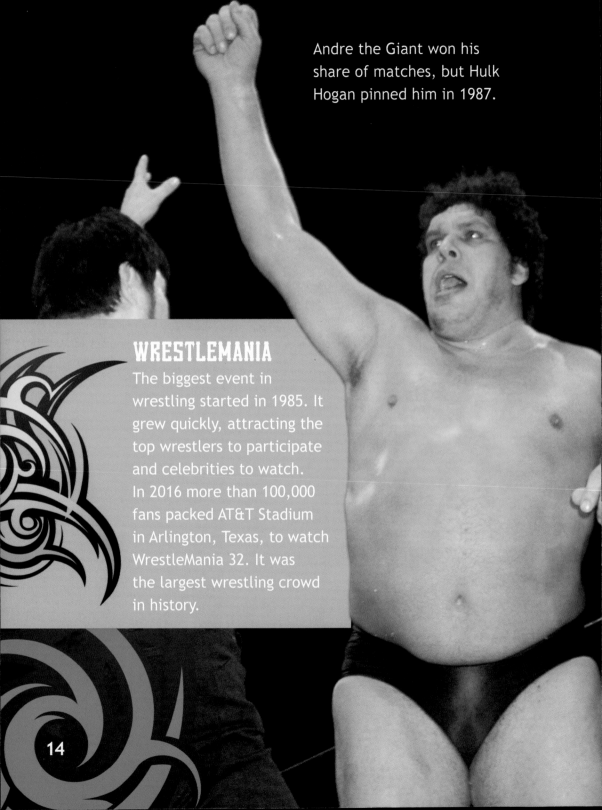

Andre the Giant won his share of matches, but Hulk Hogan pinned him in 1987.

WRESTLEMANIA

The biggest event in wrestling started in 1985. It grew quickly, attracting the top wrestlers to participate and celebrities to watch. In 2016 more than 100,000 fans packed AT&T Stadium in Arlington, Texas, to watch WrestleMania 32. It was the largest wrestling crowd in history.

SEVEN

HULK HOGAN vs ANDRE THE GIANT (1987)

Hulk Hogan and Andre the Giant were longtime friends. But that changed in 1987. Andre demanded a shot to take Hogan's title. The two met at WrestleMania 3. It was a tense, back-and-forth battle. Hogan "Hulked up," lifted the 520-pound (236-kg) giant, and slammed him to the mat. The crowd roared as the referee counted, "1 . . . 2 . . . 3!"

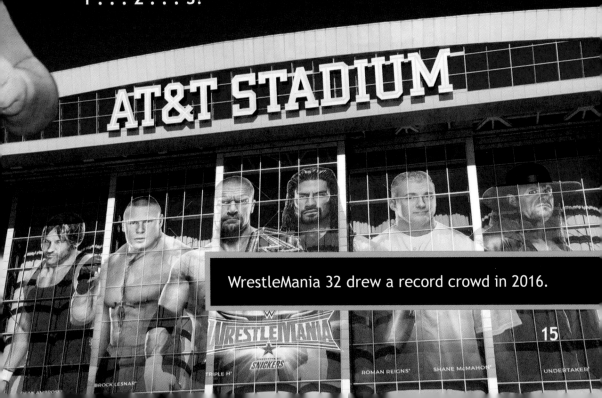

WrestleMania 32 drew a record crowd in 2016.

SIX

TRIPLE H vs THE UNDERTAKER (2012)

Triple H and The Undertaker were two of WWE's biggest stars at WrestleMania 28. Add in guest referee Shawn Michaels and a steel cage, and it was a recipe for a legendary match. Triple H and The Undertaker battled inside and outside the cage. Triple H used steel chairs and even a sledgehammer in the brawl. But it wasn't enough. The Undertaker finished him off with a crushing Tombstone Piledriver.

Shawn Michaels, *left*, and The Undertaker help Triple H out of the ring after their epic cage match.

Jeff Hardy shows his ladder-climbing skills, but Edge and Christian won the three-way tag-team bout at WrestleMania 17.

FIVE

EDGE AND CHRISTIAN vs THE DUDLEY BOYZ vs THE HARDY BOYZ (2001)

Singles matches usually get the most attention. But the most memorable match of WrestleMania 17 was a three-way tag-team bout. Two tag-team belts were on the line at this tables, ladders, and chairs (TLC) match. Fans roared at the high-flying moves and huge crashes. Edge and Christian came out on top. Edge held back the Hardy Boyz and the Dudley Boyz while Christian grabbed the belts.

FOUR

CM PUNK vs
JOHN CENA (2011)

In 2011 John Cena was the WWE's biggest star. But Cena got no love from the fans at 2011's Money in the Bank event in Chicago. Instead the fans cheered for Chicago native CM Punk. Cena dominated early. He hit CM Punk with two Attitude Adjustments. Yet he couldn't complete the pin. CM Punk roared back, pinning Cena and claiming the WWE Championship.

CM Punk, *left*, has John Cena cornered in a 2011 match.

THREE

RICKY "THE DRAGON" STEAMBOAT vs RIC FLAIR (1989)

Two of the biggest stars in the National Wrestling Alliance (NWA) faced off at the Chi-Town Rumble. Fans loved Ricky "The Dragon" Steamboat. And they loved to hate Ric Flair. The two put on an epic match. It was filled with high-flying drama, twists, and turns. Steamboat came out on top to claim the NWA World Heavyweight title.

Ricky Steamboat was back in the ring 20 years after his epic battle with Ric Flair.

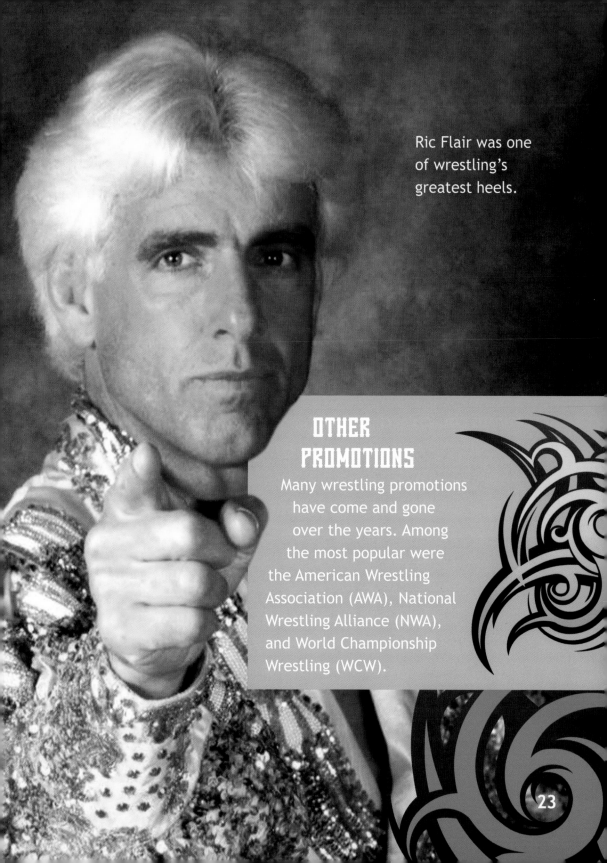

Ric Flair was one of wrestling's greatest heels.

OTHER PROMOTIONS

Many wrestling promotions have come and gone over the years. Among the most popular were the American Wrestling Association (AWA), National Wrestling Alliance (NWA), and World Championship Wrestling (WCW).

TWO

THE ROCK vs "STONE COLD" STEVE AUSTIN (2001)

WWE's "Attitude Era" was a golden age for pro wrestling. At its peak in 2001, there were no stars bigger than The Rock and "Stone Cold" Steve Austin. Their WWE title match at WrestleMania 17 is the stuff of legend. The bloody brawl spilled out into the crowd. It ended with Austin pounding The Rock over and over with a steel chair and covering up for the pin and the belt.

"Stone Cold" Steve Austin has The Rock on his back at WrestleMania 17.

ONE

THE UNDERTAKER vs SHAWN MICHAELS (2009)

The Undertaker and Shawn Michaels had an epic clash at WrestleMania 25. Michaels has been called the greatest all-around wrestler in history. And The Undertaker was a giant who had never lost at WrestleMania. Their clash left fans breathless. Time and again, each man pulled off crushing signature moves. And time and again, his opponent escaped what seemed like a sure pin.

Shawn Michaels delivers a flying elbow to The Undertaker during their infamous match at WrestleMania 25.

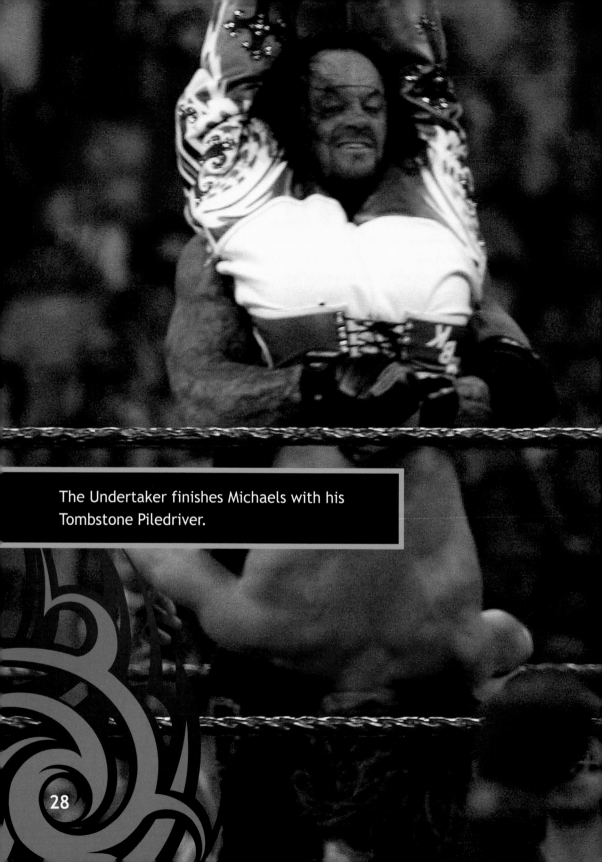

The Undertaker finishes Michaels with his Tombstone Piledriver.

The match dragged on. The Undertaker pulled off his second Tombstone Piledriver of the match. This time Michaels could not kick out of the pin. The Undertaker's streak lived on.

The two men met a year later at WrestleMania 26 in a classic rematch. The Undertaker won again, ending Michaels's legendary WWE career.

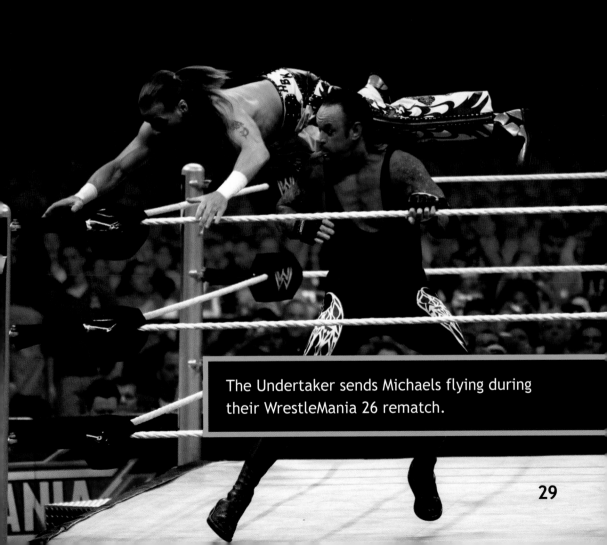

The Undertaker sends Michaels flying during their WrestleMania 26 rematch.

GLOSSARY

BABYFACE
A wrestler seen as a good guy; also called a face.

HEEL
A wrestler seen as a villain.

MAIN EVENT
The biggest match of a wrestling show, usually the final match of the night.

RIVALRY
A long-standing, intense, and often emotional competition between two people or teams.

SIGNATURE MOVE
A move for which a wrestler is best known.

TLC MATCH
Short for "tables, ladders, and chairs," a match in which opposing teams use these objects to try to reach a belt suspended above the ring.

FOR MORE INFORMATION

BOOKS

Kortemeier, Todd. *Superstars of WWE*. Mankato, MN: Amicus High
  Interest, 2016.

Scheff, Matt. *Pro Wrestling's Greatest Rivalries*. Minneapolis, MN:
  Abdo Publishing, 2017.

WEBSITES

To learn more about pro wrestling,
visit booklinks.abdopublishing.com. These links
are routinely monitored and updated to provide
the most current information available.

INDEX

ABOUT THE AUTHOR

Matt Scheff is an artist and author living in Alaska. He enjoys mountain climbing, deep-sea fishing, and curling up with his two Siberian huskies to watch wrestling.